101 Things To Do With A Tortilla

101 Things To Do With A Tortilla

BY
STEPHANIE ASHCRAFT
AND DONNA KELLY

Gibbs Smith, Publisher
Salt Lake City

First Edition
12 11 10 09 08   20 19 18 17 16 15 14 13 12 11 10 9 8 7 6

Published by
Gibbs Smith, Publisher
P.O. Box 667
Layton, Utah 84041

Orders: 1.800.748.5439
www.gibbs-smith.com

Designed by Kurt Wahlner
Printed and bound in Korea

Library of Congress Cataloging-in-Publication Data

Ashcraft, Stephanie.
101 things to do with a tortilla / Stephanie Ashcraft and Donna Kelly.—1st ed.
    p. cm.
ISBN-13: 978-1-58685-469-0
ISBN-10: 1-58685-469-0
1. Tortillas. I. Title: One hundred and one things to do with a tortilla. II. Kelly, Donna. III.
Title.

TX770.T65A84 2004
641.8'2—dc22
                    2004020953

With love and admiration
to the domestic goddesses who
have inspired me: Carol, Carol
Ann, Ruby, Glad, Joann, Lisa,
June, Karen, Noretta, Sandy, and
especially for Anne, Kathleen,
and Amelia. —D. K.

Thanks to all my family for
their support, and to my college
roommates—Felicia, who
introduced me to cooking
with tortillas, and Royleane, who
got me excited about cooking
in the first place. —S. A.

CONTENTS

Breakfast

Main Dishes

Mexican Favorites

Desserts

HELPFUL HINTS

I. Corn tortillas come in a standard 6-inch size. Generally, they must be cooked before being eaten. Heat an 8-inch or larger skillet on the stove top and lay a tortilla on the hot pan. With a spatula, flip the tortilla every 30–45 seconds, or until lightly toasted but bendable.

2. Flour tortillas come ready to eat in a variety of shapes and sizes. In this book, we refer to flour tortillas in three sizes: small (6–7 inch diameter, often called "taco size"); medium (8–10 inch diameter, and most common size); and large (11–14 inch diameter, often called "burrito size").

3. Flour tortillas come in a variety of thicknesses, including an extra thick version called "gordita-style." These are heavier than average flour tortillas, and are often used in recipes that require baking, such as for main dishes.

4. Flour tortillas often come in a variety of flavors, such as wheat, tomato, or spinach. These may be substituted for regular flour tortillas in any recipe, but baking times may need to be adjusted, and the flavor will be a little different.

5. To prevent tortillas from cracking or breaking, soften them in the microwave before using. Place up to 4 tortillas at a time on a plate and cover with a paper towel. Microwave 20–30 seconds, or until tortillas are soft and bendable. Keep covered with paper towel until ready to use.

6. Tortillas store well in the refrigerator for about 2 weeks, or in the freezer 2–3 months. Always store opened tortillas in an airtight container.

7. Rolling styles for tortillas vary according to each recipe. Generally, jelly roll style means rolling the tortilla in a tight roll with both ends open. Burrito style means folding the ends in and then rolling the tortilla in a large roll, with no openings.

8. The first time you try baking a recipe, check the food 3–5 minutes before its minimum cooking time ends—each oven heats differently, so cooking time can vary.

9. For the health conscious, low-fat or light ingredients can be used in all recipes.

APPETIZERS

FOOTBALL BEAN DIP

I can (16 ounces)	**refried beans**
$2/3$ cup	**sour cream**
$1/3$ cup	**Miracle Whip**
2 tablespoons	**taco seasoning**
2 cups	**shredded lettuce**
2	**Roma tomatoes,** chopped
2	**green onions,** sliced
I can (2.25 ounces)	**sliced black olives**
I cup	**grated cheddar cheese**
I bag (16 ounces)	**tortilla chips**

Spread refried beans on bottom of an 8 x 8-inch pan. In a bowl, mix sour cream, Miracle Whip, and taco seasoning together. Spread over beans. Layer lettuce, tomatoes, green onions, olives, and cheese over top. Stand a line of tortilla chips around the sides of the pan as a garnish. Place remaining chips in a serving bowl. Makes 6–8 servings.

PEPPER JELLY BITES

6	**medium flour tortillas**
6 tablespoons	**cream cheese,** softened
6 tablespoons	**jalapeño pepper jelly**
I cup	**finely chopped pecans**

Cut each tortilla into a 6-inch square, then spread with I tablespoon cream cheese. Spread I tablespoon jelly over cream cheese, then sprinkle each tortilla with 2 tablespoons pecans. Roll up jelly roll style. Wrap individually with clear plastic wrap and refrigerate at least I hour. When ready to serve, remove plastic wrap and slice into I-inch rolls. Makes 36 bites.

SMOKED SALMON TRIANGLES

4 tablespoons	**butter,** divided
4	**medium flour tortillas**
I package (8 ounces)	**cream cheese,** softened
$^1/_2$ pound	**thinly sliced smoked salmon**
2	**medium tomatoes,** thinly sliced
I	**medium purple onion,** thinly sliced

Melt I tablespoon butter in a frying pan over low heat. Cook I tortilla until light golden brown and crisp on one side only. Remove and cool. Repeat with remaining tortillas. Divide cream cheese into four equal parts and spread over each tortilla on the noncrisp side. Then equally divide and add salmon, tomatoes, and onion. Cut each tortilla into 6 triangle wedges. Chill before serving. Garnish with freshly chopped parsley. Makes 24 triangles.

TORTILLA PINWHEELS

2 packages (8 ounces each) **cream cheese,** softened
2 tablespoons **mustard**
6 **large flour tortillas**
2 pounds **thinly sliced deli turkey**
4 cups **chopped fresh spinach**
1 **red bell pepper,** finely chopped
2 cups **grated cheese,** any type

Combine cream cheese and mustard. Spread $1/3$ cup cream cheese mixture over each tortilla. Layer turkey, spinach, pepper, and cheese onto half of each tortilla. Roll up jelly roll style. Wrap individually in plastic wrap and chill at least 1 hour. Slice each roll into 2-inch pieces and arrange on a platter. Serve chilled. Makes 24 pinwheels.

TORTILLA GARNISHES

Tortilla Matchsticks:
With a pizza cutter, slice 2 medium flour tortillas into very thin match-stick pieces. Spread on a baking sheet and bake 5–6 minutes at 400 degrees. Stir. Return to oven 3–5 minutes more. Matchsticks should be crisp and golden brown. Cool. Makes 2 cups.

Tortilla Crisps:
With a pizza cutter, cut 3 corn or 2 medium flour tortillas into small rectangles. Heat canola oil in a small frying pan over medium heat. Add a small amount of tortilla rectangles to pan. They will cook quickly. Cool on a plate covered with a paper towel. Blot carefully to remove excess oil. Makes 2 cups.

Tortilla Confetti:
Purchase flour tortillas of different colors at the deli section of a grocery store. With kitchen scissors or a pizza cutter, cut 2 medium tortillas into tiny squares. Use as they are, or follow Tortilla Matchsticks directions above for crispy tortilla confetti. Makes 2 cups.

Migas (Tortilla Crumbs):
Using the leftover tortilla crumbs at the bottom of a bag of tortilla chips, crush with a rolling pin or fork. Sprinkle over main dishes, salads, or soups as an easy last-minute garnish.

16

TORTILLA SUSHI ROLLS

2	**medium flour tortillas**
4 tablespoons	**cream cheese,** softened
I cup	**cooked white rice**
$^1/_2$ cup	**cooked crab meat**
$^1/_2$	**avocado,** sliced lengthwise into eight strips
2 tablespoons	**finely diced green onion** or **green pepper**
$^1/_2$ cup	**sour cream,** mixed with
2 teaspoons	**Tabasco sauce**

Cut tortilla to form a 6-inch square and warm in microwave until just
softened. Spread cream cheese in a thin layer over entire tortilla. Spoon
rice over half of tortilla. Place crab meat, avocado, and green onion
lengthwise over rice. Roll up tightly, jelly roll style. Cut into I-inch
pieces. Lay pieces flat on a baking sheet. Drizzle with sour cream
and Tabasco sauce mixture. Broil 3–5 minutes. Store leftovers in
refrigerator. Makes 12 rolls.

SOUTHWEST EGG ROLLS

12 **corn tortillas**
canola oil, for frying
2 cups **shredded cabbage**
2 cups **chopped spinach**
2 tablespoons **butter**
$1/2$ cup **corn**
$1/2$ cup **cooked black beans**
1 cup **grated pepper jack cheese**
1 small jar **sweet-and-sour sauce**

Cut tortillas into 6-inch squares and warm in microwave 60 seconds on a plate covered with a dishcloth.

Heat about 2 inches of oil in a small saucepan over medium heat.

In a small frying pan, saute cabbage and spinach in butter until just limp, not browned. Remove from heat and mix in corn, black beans, and cheese. Place 2 tablespoons of mixture on a tortilla and roll into an egg roll shape. Place seam-side down in hot oil in saucepan. Cook until golden brown on both sides. Serve hot with sweet-and-sour sauce for dipping. Makes 12 egg rolls.

SPINACH AND CHEESE TRIANGLES

1 cup	**chopped green onion**
1/2 cup	**butter,** melted
2 tablespoons	**minced garlic**
1 bag (16 ounces)	**frozen chopped spinach,** thawed and drained
2 cups	**crumbled feta cheese** or **queso fresco**
2	**eggs,** beaten
6	**large, thin flour tortillas**

Preheat oven to 350 degrees. Saute green onion in 1/4 cup butter for 1 minute. Add garlic and saute 2 minutes more. Add spinach and stir frequently until all moisture evaporates. Remove from heat. Stir in cheese and eggs.

Cut tortillas into 3 x 10-inch strips (about three per tortilla). Place 2 tablespoons spinach mixture on one end of a strip, and fold into a triangle, like folding a flag. Place on baking sheet, seam-side down. Brush each tortilla with melted butter. Bake 20 minutes, or until light golden brown. Makes 18 triangles.

TORTILLA FLATS

12	**gordita-style medium flour tortillas**
1 container (8 ounces)	**spreadable garlic-and-herb cheese**
	chopped vegetables and meat

Using 2-inch-round cookie cutters, cut circles out of tortillas.* Place 4 circles on a plate and microwave 30 seconds. Remove tortillas and press flat with a dishtowel to remove any bubbles. Wipe moisture off plate. Replace tortilla rounds on plate. Microwave another 30 seconds, or until crisp, but not brown.

Spread a thin layer of cheese on top of each round. Then place chopped vegetables and meat, as desired. Recommended meats are smoked chicken chunks or grilled shrimp. Recommended vegetables are chopped fresh green and red chiles, grated jicama with lime and seasoned salt, or sliced cherry tomatoes. Makes 48 appetizers.

*Festive holiday cookie cutters such as stars or hearts may be used.

GUACAMOLE AND CHIPS

2	**large ripe avocados,** peeled and seeded
I tablespoon	**lime juice**
2 tablespoons	**finely chopped onion**
¼ teaspoon	**salt**
	tortilla chips

Mash avocados right before serving. Stir in lime juice, onion, and salt. Serve with tortilla chips or as aside for tacos or burritos. Makes 2 cups guacamole.

NEVER-FAIL NACHOS

8 cups **tortilla chips**
2 cups **grated cheddar cheese**

Preheat oven to 475 degrees. Spread tortilla chips in a 9 x 13-inch pan
or on a baking sheet. Sprinkle cheese over top. Place in oven on center
rack 1–3 minutes, or until cheese is melts. Remove from oven and top
with desired toppings as listed below. Return pan to center of oven and
broil 3–5 minutes, or until bubbly and hot. Makes 3–5 servings.

College Survival variation: Spread 1 can (16 ounces) refried beans
evenly over chips and cheese. Broil as directed above. Remove from
oven and garnish with salsa, guacamole, and/or sour cream, if desired.

Barbecue Chicken variation: Dice 2 barbecued chicken breasts.
Sprinkle over chips and cheese. Chop 1/2 red onion and sprinkle over top.
Broil as directed above. Remove from oven, drizzle spicy barbecue sauce
on top, and garnish with chopped cilantro and tomatoes.

Taco-style variation: Cook 1/2 pound ground beef seasoned with
chili powder and garlic salt, to taste. Spoon meat on top of chips and
cheese. Broil as directed above. Remove from oven and sprinkle with
shredded lettuce, chopped tomatoes, and salsa.

QUESADILLAS
AND WRAPS

BEAN 'N' CHEESE QUESADILLAS

I can (16 ounces)	**refried beans**
10	**medium flour tortillas**
$1^2/_3$ cups	**taco-blend grated cheese**
$3/_4$ cup	**green taco sauce**
$1/_2$ cup	**chopped green onion**

Heat refried beans and spread evenly over 5 tortillas. On each tortilla, sprinkle $1/_3$ cup cheese over bean layer, followed by 2 tablespoons taco sauce and some green onion. Place remaining 5 tortillas over top. Cook over medium heat in a frying pan until light golden brown. Flip and toast other side. Cut quesadillas into 6 wedges with a pizza cutter. Serve with fresh salsa and/or guacamole. Makes 3–5 servings.

TOMATO OLIVE QUESADILLAS

I can (2.25 ounces) **chopped olives**
I cup **chopped green onion**
I **medium tomato,** chopped
I cup **grated mozzarella cheese**
I cup **grated cheddar cheese**
12 **small flour tortillas**

Evenly divide and layer the olives, onion, tomato, and cheeses on top of 6 tortillas; then place remaining 6 tortillas over top. Lightly toast over medium heat in a frying pan. Turn over every 30 seconds until tortilla is golden brown on both sides. Cut each tortilla into 6 wedges with a pizza cutter. Serve with guacamole, sour cream, and/or salsa. Makes 4–6 servings.

BLT WRAPS

2	**medium wheat tortillas**
2 tablespoons	**mayonnaise or Miracle Whip**
4 to 6	**slices bacon,** cooked
I cup	**shredded lettuce**
I	**medium tomato,** diced

Place tortillas on plates. Spread mayonnaise over each tortilla. Divide
bacon and layer over center of each tortilla. Sprinkle lettuce and tomato
over top. Fold in the ends of each tortilla, then roll in the sides to form a
burrito-style wrap. Makes I–2 servings.

ITALIAN ROAST BEEF WRAPS

2	**large flour tortillas**
6 to 8	**slices roast beef**
2	**slices Provolone cheese,** cut in half
I cup	**shredded lettuce**
I	**medium tomato,** chopped
$^1/_4$	**medium red** or **yellow onion,** thinly sliced
2 to 3 tablespoons	**Italian salad dressing**

Place tortillas on microwave-safe plates. Divide roast beef and lay over each tortilla. Lay cheese halves from top to bottom in the center of each tortilla. Microwave each tortilla 45–55 seconds, or until cheese melts. Divide lettuce, tomato, and onion evenly over melted cheese. Drizzle dressing over top. Fold in the ends of each tortilla, then roll in the sides to form a burrito-style wrap. Makes 1–2 servings.

MANDARIN CHICKEN WRAPS

2 **boneless, skinless chicken breasts**
oriental seasoning or **cumin**
olive or **vegetable oil**
salt and pepper, to taste
4 **large flour tortillas**
I package (8 ounces) **cream cheese,** softened
I can (8 ounces) **mandarin oranges,** drained
¹/₃ cup **chopped green onion**
I cup **chow mein noodles**
8 **red lettuce leaves**

Season chicken with your favorite oriental seasoning or cumin. Brown chicken breasts in a small amount of oil until chicken is completely cooked. Season with salt and pepper. Remove chicken from pan. Spread cream cheese over each tortilla. Using two forks, shred chicken, and then divide evenly over tortillas, leaving at least I inch uncovered on one side. Sprinkle oranges, onion, and chow mein noodles over chicken. Lay lettuce over top. Fold in the ends of each tortilla, then roll in the sides to form a burrito-style wrap. Serve immediately or wrap individually in plastic wrap and refrigerate for later use. Makes 2–4 servings.

SWISS TURKEY SPINACH WRAPS

  1 **large avocado,** peeled and seeded*
  5 **large spinach tortillas**
 10 **slices turkey breast lunch meat**
  5 **slices Swiss cheese**
  2 **medium tomatoes,** diced
3 cups **shredded lettuce**

Mash avocado with a fork. Stir a pinch of salt into avocado, and then spread evenly over tortillas. Lay 2 turkey slices over tortilla, covering tortilla as much as possible. Cut each slice of cheese in half; then lay over meat. Sprinkle tomato and lettuce in center of each tortilla. Roll tortilla jelly roll style and secure with a toothpick. Serve immediately or wrap individually in plastic wrap and refrigerate for later use. Makes 3–5 servings.

*2 small avocados may be substituted.

TERIYAKI FISH WRAPS

3 cans (8 ounces each)	**tuna** or **other white fish fillets**
1 jar (12 ounces)	**teriyaki marinade**
2 tablespoons	**canola oil**
$3/4$ cup	**sour cream**
$3/4$ cup	**honey mustard salad dressing**
8	**large flour tortillas**
2 cups	**chopped lettuce**
1	**medium red onion,** finely diced
2	**medium tomatoes,** diced

Cut fish fillets into chunks and marinate in teriyaki sauce at least 2 hours. In a frying pan, saute fish in oil until heated through. Combine sour cream and dressing. Warm tortillas in microwave. Spread dressing mixture on tortillas. Add fish, lettuce, onion, and tomato. Fold in the ends of each tortilla then roll in the sides to form a burrito-style wrap. Makes 6–8 servings.

VARIATION: Use chicken instead of fish.

TUNA MELT TRIANGLES

3	**medium, gordita-style flour tortillas**
I can (12 ounces)	**tuna,** drained
I package (8 ounces)	**cream cheese,** softened
I cup	**finely grated mozzarella cheese**
1/2 cup	**Parmesan cheese**
I tablespoon	**dried parsley**
I teaspoon	**lemon juice**

Cut each tortilla into quarters. Place triangles directly onto oven rack and bake 6–8 minutes at 350 degrees. Turn triangles over and bake another 3–5 minutes, or until crisp and golden brown. Remove from oven.

Mix remaining ingredients together; spread evenly on each tortilla triangle. Place on a baking sheet and put on center oven rack. Broil 2–3 minutes, or until mixture is bubbly and golden brown. Makes 2–3 servings.

OPEN-FACE PESTO QUESADILLAS

2 cups **grated cheddar cheese**
4 **medium flour tortillas**
I small jar (6 ounces) **pesto sauce**
2 **small tomatoes,** thinly sliced
I **cooked chicken breast,**
thinly sliced (optional)
$^1/_2$ cup **pine nuts** or **slivered almonds**

Preheat oven to 350 degrees. Sprinkle cheese over 2 tortillas and place remaining tortillas on top. Place in oven directly on rack and bake 6–8 minutes. Remove from oven and press tortilla flat with a clean dishtowel to remove any air bubbles. Turn over and bake 3–5 minutes more. Remove from oven. Layer pesto sauce, tomatoes, chicken, if desired, and nuts over each tortilla. Broil in oven until hot and bubbly. Makes 2–4 servings.

CHICKEN CAESAR WRAPS

2 **chicken breasts,** cooked and chilled
6 cups **chopped romaine lettuce**
$1/2$ cup **Caesar salad dressing**
1 cup **grated Parmesan cheese**
6 **large flour tortillas**

Cut chicken breasts into small cubes. Toss lettuce in dressing. Place lettuce, cheese, and chicken evenly over tortillas. Fold in the ends of each tortilla, then roll in the sides to form a burrito-style wrap. Makes 4–6 servings.

CHICKEN QUESADILLA STACKS

1	**red pepper,** chopped
1 pint (16 ounces)	**sour cream**
3 cups	**cooked shredded chicken**
2 cups	**grated zucchini**
2 cups	**grated green pepper**
6 tablespoons	**butter,** divided
8	**medium flour tortillas**
2 cups	**grated Monterey Jack cheese**
	sour cream
	salsa

Preheat oven to 350 degrees. Puree red pepper in a blender; then combine with sour cream in a bowl and set aside.

Saute chicken, zucchini, and green pepper in 2 tablespoons butter. Cook 5 minutes, or until vegetables are tender. Remove from heat and drain excess liquid. Add sour cream sauce.

Place 2 tortillas on a baking sheet. Spread $1/2$ tablespoon butter on each tortilla and ladle $2/3$ cup chicken mixture over top, spreading to the edges. Sprinkle with $1/4$ cup cheese. Repeat this process 3 more times, ending with cheese on top. Bake 15 to 20 minutes, or until heated through and bubbly. Cut each tortilla stack into 4 wedges. Serve with a dollop of sour cream and salsa. Makes 6–8 servings.

KIDS AND SNACKS

HAPPY CLOWN FACES

3 tablespoons	**butter**
6	**corn tortillas**
6 tablespoons	**cinnamon sugar**
I container (8 ounces)	**whipped cream cheese,** softened
	sliced fruits
	coconut
	nuts
	chocolate chips

In a small frying pan, saute each tortilla in $^1/2$ tablespoon butter until light golden brown and crisp. Remove, sprinkle with cinnamon sugar, and cool. Spread lightly with cream cheese. Let each child make a face by placing fruit, coconut, nuts, and chocolate chips over cream cheese. Makes 6 faces.

TORTILLA SNOWFLAKES

6 **large, thin flour tortillas**
I cup **chocolate nut spread** (like Nutella)
I cup **powdered sugar**

Place a tortilla in the microwave 20–30 seconds, or until softened. Remove from microwave and fold in half, then fold in half again. Cut a design into folded tortilla, just like cutting a paper snowflake. Open up, place tortilla snowflake on a plate, and microwave 30 seconds. Take tortilla off the plate, wipe off any excess moisture, and let cool. Tortilla should be crisp but not brown. Place tortilla on a sheet of wax paper. Using a small paintbrush, paint chocolate spread on tortilla. Dust each snowflake generously with powdered sugar. Makes 6 snowflakes.

TORTILLA ELEPHANT EARS

2 cups **canola oil,** for frying
8 **medium, gordita-style flour tortillas**
2 tablespoons **cinnamon**
1 cup **sugar**

Heat oil over medium heat in a frying pan. Fry each tortilla in oil, turning over until light golden brown on each side. Do not crisp. Mix together cinnamon and sugar. Spread sugar mixture on a large plate. Using tongs, remove tortilla from pan and immediately press each side of tortilla into sugar mixture. Serve warm. Makes 6–8 servings.

VARIATION: Use festive holiday cookie cutters to cut holes in tortilla before frying. For Halloween, cut a jack-o'-lantern face in tortilla before frying.

CREAMY FRUIT ROLL-UPS

2 tablespoons **cream cheese**
1 **medium flour tortilla**
$^1/_2$ cup **finely chopped fruit**

Spread cream cheese on tortilla and sprinkle with fruit. Strawberries, bananas, crushed pineapple, berries, chopped apples, and mandarin oranges may be used. Roll up tortilla, jelly roll style. Makes 1 serving.

VARIATION: Use fruity jams instead of chopped fruit.

BANANA SPLIT ROLL

I	**medium flour tortilla**
2 tablespoons	**chocolate nut spread** (like Nutella)
2 tablespoons	**chopped nuts**
2 tablespoons	**chopped maraschino cherries**
I	**medium banana,** peeled

Spread tortilla with chocolate spread. Sprinkle nuts and cherries over top. Place banana on one edge of tortilla. Make cuts on the inside curve of the banana so that it can be straightened out. Roll tortilla up, jelly roll style. Makes I serving.

HAM-AND-CHEESE ROLL

I	**small flour tortilla**
I tablespoon	**mayonnaise,** mixed with
I teaspoon	**mustard**
I	**slice ham**
I	**individual piece string cheese**
I	**dill pickle,** cut lengthwise in quarters

Spread tortilla with mayonnaise and mustard mixture. Top with ham, string cheese, and dill pickle. Roll tortilla up with cheese and pickle in the center. Makes I serving.

VARIATION: Subsitute turkey or roast beef for the ham.

PEANUT BUTTER S'MORES

I tablespoon **peanut butter**
I **medium flour tortilla**
1/8 cup **milk chocolate chips**
1/4 cup **mini marshmallows**

Spread peanut butter over tortilla. Sprinkle remaining ingredients over top. Microwave 45 seconds. Allow to cool 3–5 minutes. Roll jelly roll style when cool. Makes I serving.

VARIATION: Substitute grated carrots, apples, raisins, bananas, or crushed pineapple for chocolate chips and marshmallows.

PIGS IN A BLANKET

1 package (8 count) **hot dogs**
4 **slices cheddar cheese**
8 **small, gordita-style flour tortillas**

Preheat oven to 425 degrees. Make a slice in each hot dog lengthwise. Insert a half slice of cheese in the center of each hot dog. Cut tortillas in half. Wrap one half around each hot dog and secure with a toothpick. Place each tortilla-wrapped hot dog on a baking sheet. Bake 10–12 minutes, or until golden brown. Makes 6–8 servings.

Soups and Salads

INSTANT CHICKEN TACO SOUP

I can (15 ounces) **whole kernel corn,** with liquid
I can (12.5 ounces) **chunk chicken,** with liquid
I can (15 ounces) **black beans,** rinsed and drained
I can (10 ounces) **diced tomatoes with green**
chile peppers, with liquid
I can (14.5 ounces) **chicken broth**
I envelope **taco seasoning mix**
I bag (12–16 ounces) **tortilla chips**
grated cheddar cheese

Combine all ingredients except tortilla chips and cheese in a medium saucepan. Bring to a light boil, and remove from heat. Crush desired amount of tortilla chips in bottom of soup bowls. Pour soup over chips. Garnish with cheese. Makes 4–6 servings.

CHICKEN ENCHILADA SOUP

2 cups	**cooked, chopped chicken breasts**
1 tablespoon	**butter**
$^1/_2$ cup	**diced green onion**
1 tablespoon	**minced garlic**
3 cups	**chicken broth**
1 can (14 ounces)	**enchilada sauce**
4	**corn tortillas**
1 cup	**sour cream**
2 cups	**grated cheddar cheese**

Saute chicken in butter. Add onion and garlic and cook until tender.
Add broth and enchilada sauce. Cut tortillas into small pieces with a
pizza cutter. Add to soup. Simmer 5–10 minutes. Add sour cream and
cheese and stir until melted. Serve hot with crushed tortilla chips as a
garnish. Makes 4–6 servings.

CREAMY TURKEY TORTILLA SOUP

10	**corn tortillas**
I can (14 ounces)	**chicken broth**
I can (15 ounces)	**green enchilada sauce**
I can (10 ounces)	**red enchilada sauce**
I teaspoon	**cumin**
2^1/$_4$ cups	**cooked, shredded turkey**
I cup	**half-and-half***
	grated cheddar cheese

Cut tortillas into ^{1}/$_2$ x 3-inch strips. In a saucepan, cook tortilla strips and chicken broth over medium heat until broth thickens and tortillas are soft. Add enchilada sauces and cumin. Mix in turkey and half-and-half. Cook until hot, but do not allow to boil. Garnish individual servings with cheese. Makes 4 servings.

*Whole milk may be substituted.

DO-IT-YOURSELF TORTILLA SOUP

12 cups **hot chicken broth**
3 cups **cooked cubed chicken**
3 cups **grated cheddar cheese**
1 cup **Tortilla Matchsticks** (see Tortilla Garnishes page 16)
4 cups **finely chopped raw vegetables,** such as avocado,
onion, green peppers, tomatoes, and olives
salsa, if desired
sour cream, if desired

Keep chicken broth simmering in a pan on the stove or in a slow cooker over high heat. Place each remaining ingredient in separate serving bowls. Have each person take an empty bowl and fill with ingredients of his or her choice. Ladle hot broth over top of ingredients and stir. Top with a handful of Tortilla Matchsticks. Serve with a dollop of salsa or sour cream, if desired. Makes 4–6 servings.

GREEN CHILE TORTILLA SOUP

I can (26 ounces) **chicken and rice soup,** condensed
2 cups **water**
I can (10 ounces) **diced tomatoes with green chiles,**
with liquid
tortilla chips
I cup **grated cheddar cheese**

Combine soup, water, and tomatoes in a medium saucepan. Bring to a boil and remove from heat. Crush tortilla chips in bottom of individual soup bowls. Pour soup over chips and sprinkle cheese over top. Makes 4 servings.

ZESTY RANCH BEAN TORTILLA SOUP

5 1/2 cups	**water**
4	**boneless, skinless chicken breasts**
I	**medium onion,** chopped
I can (16 ounces)	**kidney beans,** drained
I can (15 ounces)	**garbanzo beans,** drained
I can (16 ounces)	**pinto beans,** drained
I can (15 ounces)	**black beans,** rinsed and drained
2 cans (10 ounces each)	**diced tomatoes with green chile peppers,** with liquid
I envelope	**taco seasoning**
I envelope	**ranch dressing mix**
	tortilla chips
	grated Monterey Jack cheese

In a 4-quart soup pan, combine water and chicken, and simmer over medium-high heat 30–45 minutes, or until chicken is cooked through. Remove chicken and cut into bite-size pieces. Return chicken to the broth in pan and stir in onion, beans, tomatoes, taco seasoning, and ranch dressing mix. Simmer 20 minutes over medium-low heat, or until heated through. Serve soup over crushed tortilla chips. Garnish each individual bowl with cheese and a dollop of sour cream. Makes 8–10 servings.

FESTIVE CONFETTI SALAD

I container (16 ounces) **cottage cheese**
$^1/_4$ cup **chopped carrot**
$^1/_4$ cup **chopped onion**
$^1/_4$ cup **chopped red pepper**
$^1/_4$ cup **chopped green pepper**
I can (8 ounces) **pineapple tidbits,** drained
I tablespoon **sugar** or **sweetener,** to taste
6 cups **blue corn tortilla chips**
$^1/_2$ cup **toasted sunflower seeds**

Mix cottage cheese, vegetables, pineapple, and sugar. Spread a handful of tortilla chips on a small plate. Top with I cup mounded cottage cheese mixture. Sprinkle generously with sunflower seeds. Eat with your fingers, using tortillas as scoops. Makes 4–6 servings.

BLACK BEAN
GUACAMOLE SALAD

12	**whole tortilla chips**
4 cups	**broken tortilla chips**
3 cups	**chopped lettuce**
I can (15 ounces)	**black beans,** rinsed and drained
2 cups	**guacamole**
I cup	**sour cream,** thinned with
I tablespoon	**lime juice**
	chili powder or **paprika**

Arrange whole tortilla chips on outside edge of a large plate, pointing
out. Spread broken chips on rest of plate. Layer lettuce, black beans,
and guacamole over top. Drizzle on sour cream mixture. Sprinkle with
paprika or chili powder. Makes 4 servings.

SEAFOOD TOSTADA SALAD

1 cup	**tiny shrimp,** cooked and chilled
1 1/2 cups	**crab meat,** cooked and chilled
1	**ripe avocado,** sliced
1 cup	**chopped green onion**
1 package (8 ounces)	**frozen peas**
1/2 cup	**vinegar**
6 tablespoons	**canola oil**
1 tablespoon	**sugar** or **sweetener**
6	**corn tortilla tostada shells**
1 can (16 ounces)	**refried beans,** heated
2 cups	**grated cheddar cheese**
8 cups	**finely chopped lettuce**

Mix first eight ingredients together and set aside.

Spread each tostada shell with 1/4 cup refried beans and top with 1/3 cup cheese. Place each tostada on a plate. Stir lettuce into seafood mixture, divide into 6 servings, and mound lettuce mixture onto each tostada. Sprinkle cheese over top. Makes 6 servings.

TACO SALAD IN A TORTILLA BOWL

6 **large flour tortillas**
I pound **ground beef** or **turkey**
I tablespoon **chili powder**
I teaspoon **garlic salt**
I can (30 ounces) **refried beans,** heated
6 to 8 cups **shredded lettuce**
3 cups **chopped tomatoes**
3 cups **grated cheddar cheese**
salsa

Preheat oven to 375 degrees. Spray an empty 4- to 5-inch-diameter can or baking pan with nonstick cooking spray. Drape a tortilla over top. Bake 8–10 minutes, or until light golden brown. Let cool 5 minutes before removing tortilla from can or pan. While tortilla is baking, brown meat in spices.

Place tortilla bowls on plates. Spread beans evenly in bottom of each tortilla bowl. Spoon meat on top of beans; layer remaining ingredients over top of meat. Makes 6 servings.

LAYERED RAINBOW SALAD

2 cups	**crushed blue corn tortilla chips**
1 package (8 ounces)	**frozen peas**
6	**hard-boiled eggs,** sliced
2 cups	**thinly sliced carrots**
2 cups	**chopped red peppers**
1 cup	**chopped purple onion**
1 cup	**chopped celery**
1 cup	**mayonnaise**
$^1/_2$ cup	**sour cream**
1 tablespoon	**sugar** or **sweetener**

In an 8-inch glass trifle bowl, layer chips, peas, eggs, carrots, and red peppers. Then spread purple onion close to outside of bowl and fill center with celery. Combine mayonnaise, sour cream, and sugar, and spread over top to seal. Cover and refrigerate 1–2 hours. Serve chilled. Makes 6–8 servings.

PICNIC TACO SALAD

1 pound	**ground beef**
1 envelope	**taco seasoning**
8 cups	**shredded lettuce**
2 cups	**chopped tomatoes**
2 cups	**grated cheddar cheese**
1 can (15 ounces)	**black or pinto beans,** rinsed and drained
4 cups	**crushed corn tortilla chips**
1 small bottle (14 ounces)	**Russian salad dressing**

Brown meat and add taco seasoning according to directions. Cool.
Combine all ingredients except Russian dressing and tortilla chips.
Refrigerate 1–2 hours. Add dressing and chips right before serving.
Makes 6–8 servings.

BREAKFAST

OVERNIGHT BRUNCH ENCHILADAS

1 bag (16 ounces)	**fully-cooked cubed ham**
1/2 cup	**sliced green onion**
3/4 cup	**chopped green pepper**
10	**medium flour tortillas**
2 1/2 cups	**grated cheddar cheese,** divided
5	**large eggs,** beaten
2 cups	**half-and-half**
1/2 cup	**milk**
1 tablespoon	**flour**
1/2 teaspoon	**garlic powder**
1/2 teaspoon	**black pepper**

Stir together ham, green onion, and green pepper. Spread 1/3 cup mixture down middle of each tortilla. Sprinkle 2 tablespoons cheese over top. Roll tortillas and place them, seam-side down, in bottom of a greased 9 x 13-inch pan. Mix eggs, half-and-half, milk, flour, garlic powder, and pepper together. Pour egg mixture evenly over rolled tortillas. Cover and refrigerate overnight. Preheat oven to 350 degrees. Bake, uncovered, 50 minutes, or until egg mixture is cooked through. Sprinkle remaining cheese over enchiladas. Bake an additional 3–5 minutes, or until cheese melts. Makes 8–10 servings.

HAM-AND-CHEESE BREAKFAST BURRITOS

$3/4$ cup **cooked ham,** cubed
5 **large eggs,** beaten
I tablespoon **milk**
salt and pepper, to taste
$1/4$ cup **grated cheddar cheese**
4 **medium flour tortillas**
salsa

In a nonstick frying pan sprayed with vegetable oil, cook ham 3–4 minutes. Stir in eggs and milk. Season with salt and pepper. Scramble eggs over medium-low heat until done. Sprinkle cheese over eggs. Roll scrambled eggs in a tortilla. Serve with salsa. Makes 2–4 servings.

BREAKFAST TOSTADA

butter or **margarine**
4 **corn tortillas**
1 cup **grated cheddar cheese**
2 cups **shredded lettuce**
1 1/4 cups **cooked ham,** cubed
4 **eggs,** scrambled

Preheat oven to 400 degrees. Spread butter or margarine on one side
of each tortilla and lay tortillas butter-side up on a large baking sheet.
Bake 3–5 minutes, or until tortillas are toasted. Flip tortillas, then
sprinkle cheese over top. Bake 1–2 minutes, or until cheese melts.
Layer lettuce, ham, and scrambled eggs over top. Garnish with
chopped tomato, sliced olives, and sour cream. Makes 4 servings.

GREEN CHILE EGGS BENEDICT

8	**corn tortillas**
4 tablespoons	**butter**
2 cups	**hollandaise sauce**
4	**slices cooked ham** or **Canadian bacon**
8	**strips mild green chiles**
8	**eggs,** scrambled, poached, or fried

Saute each tortilla in $1/2$ tablespoon butter until lightly crisp and golden brown. Place 2 corn tortillas on a plate. Spread a few tablespoons of sauce on top. Top with a slice of meat, 2 strips chiles, and 2 cooked eggs. Repeat with remaining tortillas and ingredients. Ladle $1/4$ cup sauce over top. Heat each plate in microwave 90 seconds. Makes 4 servings.

OVERNIGHT BREAKFAST CASSEROLE

12 **eggs**
3 cups **milk**
I teaspoon **salt**
I teaspoon **dry mustard**
6 **medium flour tortillas,** torn into small pieces
2 cups **sausage,** cooked and crumbled
I cup **chopped onion**
I cup **chopped green peppers**
2 cups **grated cheddar** or **Swiss cheese**

Mix eggs, milk, salt, and dry mustard together. Pour I cup of egg mixture into a greased 9 x 13-inch pan. Layer half of tortilla pieces, sausage, onion, green pepper, and cheese over top. Cover with remaining egg mixture. Layer remaining ingredients over top, ending with cheese. Cover and refrigerate overnight. Bake 40–50 minutes at 350 degrees. Makes 6–8 servings.

HUEVOS RANCHEROS STACKS

12 **corn tortillas**
6 cups **enchilada sauce**
2 cups **grated cheddar cheese**
8 **eggs,** scrambled, poached, or fried
2 cups **chopped onion** or **green pepper**

Dip 3 corn tortillas in enchilada sauce to coat. Stack 3 tortillas on four separate plates. Sprinkle on some cheese. Place 2 cooked eggs on each stack. Drizzle on more sauce and sprinkle onion or green pepper over top each stack. Top with more cheese. Microwave each plate 60 seconds, or until hot and bubbling. Makes 4 servings.

COATED TORTILLA FRENCH TOAST

6 **eggs**
2 cups **milk**
I teaspoon **cinnamon**
2 teaspoons **vanilla**
6 **medium, gordita-style flour tortillas**

Mix all ingredients together except tortillas. Dip each tortilla in egg mixture and place in a frying pan with a little butter over medium heat. Cook about 30 seconds and turn over. Spread 2 tablespoons egg mixture on tortillas. Turn over again. Keep repeating this process until a layer of egg mixture coats each side of tortilla thoroughly and is golden brown and crispy. Serve as you would traditional French toast. Makes 3–4 servings.

TORTILLA QUICHES

6	**small flour tortillas**
4	**eggs**
I can (12 ounces)	**evaporated milk**
I tablespoon	**flour**
I teaspoon	**salt**
$^1/_2$ cup	**chopped cooked ham, bacon,** or **sausage**
$^1/_4$ cup	**chopped green onion**
I cup	**finely grated Swiss cheese**
	salsa
	sour cream

Preheat oven to 350 degrees. Place a tortilla in microwave 20 seconds, or until softened. Spray one side of each tortilla with nonstick cooking spray and press into 6 (10-ounce) custard baking cups. Tortilla will stick up about $^1/_2$ inch over the top.

In a small bowl, combine eggs, milk, flour, and salt together and set aside. Divide remaining ingredients into tortilla cups, end with cheese on top. Pour egg mixture over top, about $^1/_2$ cup in each, or until about $^2/_3$ full. Bake 50 minutes, or until set and lightly browned. Remove from oven and cool slightly before serving. Serve with salsa and sour cream as a garnish. Makes 4–6 individual quiches.

CONFETTI BREAKFAST BAKE

12	**corn tortillas**
I can (15 ounces)	**black beans,** rinsed and drained
I can (15 ounces)	**corn,** drained
1/2 cup	**chopped green onion**
1/2 cup	**chopped red pepper**
3 tablespoons	**chopped fresh cilantro**
I cup	**grated cheddar cheese**
2 cups	**milk** or **half-and-half**
6	**eggs,** slightly beaten

Preheat oven to 325 degrees. Arrange 6 tortillas in a lightly greased 9 x 13-inch pan. Tortillas will overlap. Cut remaining tortillas into 1-inch square pieces. Mix pieces with beans, corn, green onion, red pepper, cilantro, and half of cheese. Spoon into pan. Combine milk and eggs. Pour egg mixture over top. Sprinkle with remaining cheese. Cover and refrigerate 4 hours or overnight. Bake 60 minutes, or until eggs are set. Let stand 5 minutes before serving. Makes 6–8 servings.

HUEVOS MIGAS

1/2 cup **chopped green onion**
2 tablespoons **butter**
8 **eggs**
1 cup **milk**
1/2 cup **chopped tomato**
1 can (4 ounces) **diced green chiles,** drained
1 cup **crushed tortilla chips**

Saute onion in butter in a medium frying pan. Mix eggs and milk, and pour into pan. Scramble over medium heat until eggs are set. Add tomato and green chiles, and cook 3 minutes more. Stir in tortilla chips. Makes 4–6 servings.

CHILI CHEESE BREAKFAST BURRITO

4 **medium flour tortillas**
6 **eggs,** scrambled
I can (I5 ounces) **chili,** heated
I cup **grated pepper jack cheese**
I cup **salsa**

Heat tortillas in microwave 30 seconds, or until softened. Spread eggs, chili, cheese, and salsa evenly over each tortilla. Roll up and serve. Makes 2–4 servings.

Main Dishes

FAMILY FAVORITE
TACO CASSEROLE

I pound	**ground beef**
I	**medium onion,** finely chopped
2 cans (8 ounces each)	**tomato sauce**
I envelope	**taco seasoning**
10	**medium flour tortillas**
I can (10.5 ounces)	**cream of chicken soup,** condensed
3/4 cup	**milk**
2 cups	**grated cheddar** or **Mexican-blend cheese**

Preheat oven to 350 degrees. In a large frying pan, brown beef and onion together until meat is done and onion is translucent. Drain any excess liquid. Stir tomato sauce and taco seasoning into meat mixture.

Line bottom and sides of a greased 9 x 13-inch pan with 6 flour tortillas. Spread beef mixture over tortilla crust. Place remaining tortillas over top, cutting to fit if necessary, and covering completely. Mix together soup and milk, and pour over top. Sprinkle cheese over casserole. Cover with aluminum foil and bake 15 minutes. Uncover and bake an additional 5 minutes, or until cheese is completely melted. Makes 4–6 servings.

*Casserole can be assembled the night before and stored in the refrigerator until 10 minutes prior to baking.

SOUTHWEST HAYSTACKS

4 cups	**tortilla matchsticks** (see Tortilla Garnishes page 16)
8 cups	**cooked white** or **Spanish rice**
3 cups	**enchilada sauce**
1 can (16 ounces)	**pinto** or **black beans**
4 cups	**cooked and chopped chicken** or **beef**
2 to 3 cups	**grated cheddar cheese**
6 cups	**finely chopped lettuce**
6 cups	**assorted finely chopped vegetables,** such as green onion, avocado, tomato, black olives, and peppers

Place all the ingredients in separate bowls and serve buffet-style. Each person assembles their own "haystack" by starting with a layer of matchsticks, and then rice and sauce. Top with remaining ingredients of choice. Makes 6–8 servings.

MUSHROOM SWISS TORTILLA BAKE

I pound **mushrooms,** sliced
I cup **chopped green onion**
$^1/_2$ cup **butter**
I can (19 ounces) **enchilada sauce**
I can (15 ounces) **black beans,** with liquid
12 **corn tortillas**
I pound **Swiss cheese,** grated
sour cream
salsa

Saute mushrooms and onion in butter until limp. Blend enchilada
sauce and black beans in blender until smooth. Pour a little sauce in a
9 x 13-inch pan. Place 6 tortillas in bottom of pan. Spread half of mush-
room and onion mixture in pan over tortillas. Pour half of sauce in pan,
and sprinkle half of cheese over top. Repeat layers with remaining ingredients. Bake 40 minutes at 350 degrees, or until bubbly. Serve
with a dollop of sour cream and salsa. Makes 6–8 servings.

SOUTHWEST PIZZAS

8	**medium, gordita-style flour tortillas**
I jar (18 ounces)	**pizza sauce**
2 cups	**grated mozzarella cheese**
	pizza toppings (of choice)
I cup	**Parmesan cheese**

Preheat oven to 450 degrees. Spread 3 tablespoons pizza sauce on one side of a tortilla. Press another tortilla on top. Place directly on oven rack in oven. Bake 8 minutes. Remove from oven and press flat with a dishtowel to remove air bubbles. Turn over and bake another 2–3 minutes, or until tortillas are crisp and brown. Remove from oven and press flat again. Place on baking sheet and top with pizza sauce, mozzarella cheese, and toppings, as desired. Place in oven on center rack. Broil until toppings are bubbly and hot. Remove from oven and sprinkle with Parmesan cheese. Makes 4 pizzas.

SOUTHWEST LASAGNA

1 container (15 ounces)	**ricotta** or **cottage cheese**
1 package (10 ounces)	**frozen chopped spinach,** thawed and pressed dry
9	**medium flour tortillas,** torn into small pieces
1 can (19 ounces)	**enchilada sauce,** mixed with
1 cup	**salsa**
1 cup	**sliced black olives**
1 pound	**cooked hamburger,** seasoned with chili powder and salt
1/2 pound	**grated mozzarella cheese**
1 cup	**Parmesan cheese**

Preheat oven to 350 degrees. Spray a 9 x 13-inch pan with nonstick cooking spray. Mix ricotta or cottage cheese with spinach. Layer one-third of each ingredient, starting with tortillas, and then ricotta or cottage cheese mixture, enchilada sauce mixture, olives, hamburger, and mozzarella cheese. Repeat layers twice more. Sprinkle Parmesan over top. Bake 40–50 minutes, or until heated through. Makes 8–10 servings.

BLACK BEAN CASSEROLE

2 cans (7 ounces each) **diced green chiles**
2 cups **frozen corn**
1 cup **sour cream**
10 **medium flour tortillas,** torn into pieces
2 cans (15 ounces each) **black beans,** with liquid
2 cups **grated pepper jack cheese**
2 cups **salsa**

Preheat oven to 350 degrees. Combine chiles, corn, and sour cream. In a 1 1/2- to 2-quart casserole dish, layer half of tortilla pieces, beans, sour cream mixture, cheese, and salsa. Repeat with remaining ingredients. Bake 30 minutes, or until bubbly. Makes 6 servings.

CHILI CHICKEN CASSEROLE

4	**boneless, skinless chicken breasts**
12	**corn tortillas**
2 cans (10.5 ounces each)	**cream of chicken soup,** condensed
1/2 cup	**milk**
1	**medium onion,** chopped
1 can (4 ounces)	**chopped green chiles,** with liquid
1 can (15 ounces)	**chili with beans**
2 cups	**grated Monterey Jack** or **cheddar cheese**

Preheat oven to 350 degrees. Place chicken in a greased 9 x 13-inch pan. With a pizza cutter, cut tortillas into 1-inch strips. Lay tortilla strips over chicken.

In a large bowl, combine soup, milk, onion, green chiles, and chili. Spread mixture over tortilla layer. Sprinkle cheese evenly over top. Cover with aluminum foil and bake 25 minutes. Uncover and bake an additional 20–25 minutes, or until chicken is completely cooked through. Makes 4–6 servings.

CHICKEN ROLL-UPS

4 cups **cooked cubed chicken**
I package (8 ounces) **cream cheese**
I can (4 ounces) **diced green chiles,** with liquid
I teaspoon **seasoned salt**
8 **medium, gordita-style flour tortillas**
$^1/_4$ cup **butter,** melted
I can (10.5 ounces) **cream of chicken soup,** condensed
$^1/_2$ cup **milk**

Preheat oven to 350 degrees. Mix chicken, cream cheese, chiles, and salt. Soften a tortilla in microwave 20 seconds. Place $^1/_2$ cup chicken mixture on tortilla. Fold in the ends of tortilla then roll the sides to form a bundle. Place seam-side down in a greased 9 x 13-inch pan. Repeat for each tortilla. Brush each bundle with melted butter. Bake 30 minutes, or until golden brown. Mix soup and milk in a saucepan over medium heat. Ladle over each bundle before serving. Makes 4–6 servings.

LATTICE-TOP CHICKEN POTPIE

1	**large potato,** peeled
1	**large carrot,** peeled and sliced
1 bag (8 ounces)	**frozen peas**
2 cups	**cooked cubed chicken**
2 cans (10.5 ounces each)	**cream of chicken soup,** condensed
1 cup	**milk**
4	**large flour tortillas**

Preheat oven to 350 degrees. Cut potato into bite-size pieces. Cook in microwave 5 minutes, or until just tender but not thoroughly cooked. Add remaining ingredients except tortillas and stir. Pour into a 2-quart casserole dish.

Wet tortillas with water. Place two tortillas together and press firmly. Place on wax paper. Cut into 1-inch-wide strips with a pizza cutter. Lay on top of casserole, weaving together, lattice-style. Repeat with remaining two tortillas. Entire dish should be covered with strips. Bake 30 minutes, or until light golden brown. Makes 6–8 servings.

POLYNESIAN BUNDLES

3 cups	**frozen hash browns**
1/4 cup	**butter**
3/4 cup	**frozen peas**
1	**medium onion,** finely chopped
1 can (8 ounces)	**crushed pineapple,** with liquid
1 teaspoon	**powdered ginger**
1 tablespoon	**soy sauce**
12	**medium flour tortillas**
1 small jar	**sweet-and-sour sauce**

Preheat oven to 350 degrees.

In a skillet, brown hash browns in butter. Add peas, onion, pineapple, ginger, and soy sauce. Saute 5 minutes. Place 1/4 cup mixture onto a flour tortilla. Fold in the ends of tortilla and roll the sides to form a bundle. Spray 9 x 13-inch pan with nonstick cooking spray. Place each bundle seam-side down. Bake 15 minutes, then turn over. Bake 10 minutes more. Serve hot with sweet-and-sour sauce for dipping. Makes 6–8 servings.

SLOW COOKER BURRITO BAKE

1 pound	**lean ground beef**
1 envelope	**taco seasoning**
1	**medium onion,** chopped
1	**green pepper,** chopped
1 can (16 ounces)	**black beans,** with liquid
1 can (16 ounces)	**pinto beans,** with liquid
2 cans (10 ounces each)	**tomatoes and green chiles,** drained
10	**medium flour tortillas,** torn into pieces
4 cups	**grated cheddar cheese**

Brown ground beef and drain. Stir in taco seasoning. Layer one-third of each ingredient starting with seasoned hamburger in the order listed above in a greased 4¹/2- to 6-quart slow cooker. Repeat layers twice more. Cover and cook 6–8 hours on low heat or 3–4 hours on high heat. Makes 8 servings.

SOUTHWEST TORTA

12 **corn tortillas**
1 teaspoon **garlic powder**
1 can (15 ounces) **enchilada sauce**
1 can (15 ounces) **black** or **pinto beans,** rinsed and drained
3 cups **grated pepper jack cheese**
sour cream or **guacamole**

Spray a large deep-dish pie pan with nonstick cooking spray. Place 6
tortillas on bottom of pan, overlapping. Add garlic powder to enchilada
sauce. Layer half of sauce, beans, and cheese. Then repeat layers, starting
with remaining tortillas. Bake 12–15 minutes at 400 degrees. Let stand
5 minutes. Cut into triangle wedges to serve. Garnish with a dollop of
sour cream or guacamole. Makes 6 servings.

SWEET-AND-SOUR FAJITAS

I tablespoon	**vegetable** or **olive oil**
2	**boneless, skinless chicken breasts,** cubed
I bag (16 ounces)	**frozen oriental vegetables,** thawed and drained
$3/4$ cup	**sweet-and-sour** or **stir-fry sauce**
8	**medium flour tortillas**

Heat oil in large frying pan or wok. Add cubed chicken to hot oil, stirring frequently until chicken is thoroughly cooked. Add vegetables to chicken. Stir 2–3 minutes, or until vegetables are cooked through. Drain any excess liquid. Stir in sauce and cook 2 minutes more. Serve in warm flour tortillas. Makes 4 servings.

TEH-MEH MEAT LOAF

2	**lightly beaten eggs**
8	**corn tortillas,** pulverized in food processor
$^1/_2$ cup	**finely chopped onion**
$^1/_4$ cup	**chopped green pepper** or **green chiles**
I tablespoon	**chili powder** (optional)
I teaspoon	**salt**
2 pounds	**lean ground beef**
I cup	**ketchup**

Mix all ingredients together except ketchup. Shape into two small loaves.
Place in a 9 x 13-inch pan. Pour ketchup over top. Bake 60 minutes at 350
degrees. Makes 6–8 servings.

TORTILLA BEEF CANNELLONI

I jar (I 6 ounces)	**spaghetti sauce**
I pound	**lean ground beef**
I teaspoon	**garlic salt**
I tablespoon	**Italian seasoning**
I cup	**grated mozzarella cheese**
I2	**medium flour tortillas**
	Parmesan cheese

Spread 3 tablespoons spaghetti sauce in a 9 x 13-inch pan. Brown and drain beef. Add garlic salt, Italian seasoning, and mozzarella cheese. Cut tortillas into 6-inch squares. Place 2 tablespoons beef along one edge of a tortilla square. Roll up, jelly roll style, and place seam-side down in pan. Repeat process with each tortilla square. Pour remaining sauce over top. Bake 30 minutes at 375 degrees. Garnish with Parmesan. Makes 4–6 servings.

NACHO SLOPPY JOES

I pound	**ground turkey** or **beef**
I can (6 ounces)	**tomato paste**
I cup	**water**
I envelope	**sloppy joe seasoning mix**
I	**small bag tortilla chips**
I can (6 ounces)	**sliced olives**
2 cups	**grated cheddar cheese**

Brown and drain meat; add tomato paste, water, and seasoning.
Simmer 10 minutes, or until thick. Spread tortilla chips on individual
plates and spoon sloppy joe mixture over top. Sprinkle with sliced
olives and cheese. Makes 6 servings.

TORTILLA-CRUSTED FISH FILLETS

1	**egg** mixed with
1 tablespoon	**water**
1 cup	**seasoned bread crumbs**
1 cup	**finely crushed tortilla chips**
4 (4-ounce)	**fish fillets**
	butter

Place egg mixture, crumbs, and tortilla chips on separate plates or bowls. Dip fish fillets, one at a time, in egg mixture, bread crumbs, and crushed tortilla chips in that order. Saute each fish fillet in buttered frying pan on high heat, 1 minute on each side. Transfer fish fillets to casserole dish. Bake 20–30 minutes at 400 degrees. Makes 4 servings.

FAJITA BURGERS

6 tablespoons	**canola oil**
1 tablespoon	**chili powder**
1 teaspoon	**white pepper** (optional)
6	**medium flour tortillas**
6 ($^1/_4$-pound)	**ground beef patties**
2 cups	**sliced red, green,** and/or **yellow peppers**
6	**leaves lettuce**
1	**large tomato,** sliced
6	**slices cheddar** or **pepper jack cheese**

Heat a large frying pan or outdoor grill. Mix oil and spices in a small dish. Brush one side of each tortilla with oil mixture. Saute or grill each tortilla until slightly crisp but not hard, about 30 seconds each side. Cook or grill patties, cut them in half, and set aside. Saute or grill sliced peppers until just cooked, not limp. To assemble burger, place 2 halves of burger lengthwise down the center of a tortilla. Add some peppers, lettuce, tomato, and cheese over top. Fold tortilla in half to form a giant taco-looking burger. Makes 6 servings.

VARIATION: Substitute a chicken breast or veggie burger patty for the ground beef.

TORTILLA SPINACH AND CHEESE CANNELLONI

I jar (16 ounces) **Alfredo sauce**
I package (10 ounces) **frozen chopped spinach**
I teaspoon **garlic salt**
I tablespoon **Italian seasoning**
I cup **grated mozzarella cheese**
I cup **ricotta cheese**
12 **medium flour tortillas**
I **egg**
Parmesan cheese, for garnish

Spread 3 tablespoons Alfredo sauce in a lightly greased 9 x 13-inch pan.

Saute spinach in a frying pan. Stir in garlic salt, Italian seasoning, mozzarella and ricotta cheeses, and egg.

Cut tortillas into 6-inch squares. Place 2 tablespoons mixture along one edge of a tortilla square. Roll up and place seam-side down in pan. Repeat for each tortilla square. Pour remaining sauce over tortillas. Bake 30 minutes at 375 degrees. Garnish with Parmesan cheese. Makes 6 servings.

VEGETARIAN TACO CASSEROLE

I can (15 ounces) **black beans,** drained and rinsed
I can (15 ounces) **ranchero-style pinto beans,** with liquid
1 cup **salsa**
$^1/_2$ cup **sour cream**
2 teaspoons **chili powder**
3 cups **crushed tortilla chips**
2 cups **grated cheddar cheese**
2 cups **shredded lettuce**
I **medium tomato,** chopped

Mix beans, salsa, sour cream, and chili powder. Layer half of bean mixture, chips, and cheese in that order. Repeat layers. Bake 20–30 minutes, or until bubbly, at 350 degrees. Serve topped with lettuce and tomato. Makes 6 servings.

Mexican Favorites

CHICKEN SOFT TACOS

4	**boneless, skinless chicken breasts**
I tablespoon	**vegetable oil**
I	**medium onion,** chopped
I jar (16 ounces)	**chunky salsa**
2 tablespoons	**taco seasoning**
1 1/2 cups	**cheddar** or **Monterey Jack cheese**
10 to 12	**small flour tortillas**

Place chicken in a saucepan and add enough water to cover. Bring to a boil. Simmer over medium-high heat 30 minutes, or until chicken is easy to shred. Reserve 1/2 cup chicken broth from pan where chicken cooked. Shred chicken using two forks, and set aside.

Heat oil in a frying pan over medium heat. Add onion to oil and cook until translucent. Stir chicken, salsa, taco seasoning, and 1/2 cup reserved chicken broth into onion. Simmer, uncovered, over low heat 25 minutes, or until thick. Sprinkle cheese over chicken and serve in warm flour tortillas. Garnish with sour cream or guacamole. Makes 4–6 servings.

*If starting recipe with frozen chicken, boil chicken 45 minutes, or until it is ready to shred.

SHREDDED BEEF TACOS

2 pounds	**round steak**
2 tablespoons	**minced garlic**
1 tablespoon	**chili powder**
1 tablespoon	**beef broth granules**
12	**taco shells**
2	**tomatoes,** chopped
2 cups	**grated cheddar cheese**
1/2	**head iceberg lettuce,** finely shredded
	salsa

Remove visible fat from meat. Place in a lightly greased $3^1/2$- to 5-quart slow cooker. Add garlic. Cover and cook on low heat 6–8 hours. Shred meat using two forks. Add chili powder and beef broth granules. Leave in slow cooker another 30–60 minutes, stirring as necessary to remove moisture. Set out remaining ingredients in separate bowls and let individuals assemble their own tacos. Makes 8–10 servings.

CHICKEN FLAUTAS

18	**corn tortillas**
2 cans (10 ounces each)	**white chicken meat***
I teaspoon	**cumin**
I cup	**grated Monterey Jack cheese**
I can (4 ounces)	**diced green chiles**
	oil

Soften tortillas in microwave 60 seconds. Remove and cover with a dishtowel to keep tortillas warm and soft. Mix all remaining ingredients except oil.

Heat oil I inch deep in a small frying pan over medium heat. Place 2 tablespoons chicken mixture in a tortilla, spread vertically about I inch from center on one side of tortilla. Roll up jelly roll style. Using tongs, hold seam-side down for about 60 seconds in hot oil. Release and let cook 2–3 minutes more, or until crisp and brown. Roll each tortilla and repeat process. Garnish with guacamole, salsa, or sour cream. Makes 6–8 servings.

*2 cups diced cooked chicken may be substituted.

SPICY PORK TACOS

3- to 4-pound **boneless pork loin roast**
$1/4$ teaspoon **garlic salt**
1 can (10 ounces) **hot green enchilada sauce**
10 to 12 **medium flour tortillas**

Place roast in a greased $3^1/2$- to 5-quart slow cooker. Sprinkle roast with garlic salt and pour enchilada sauce over top. Cover and cook on low heat 8–10 hours. An hour before serving, shred meat using two forks and continue to cook on low heat, uncovered, for remaining time. Serve in warm flour tortillas with your favorite taco toppings. Makes 8–10 servings.

CHICKEN ENCHILADA CASSEROLE

12	**corn tortillas**
I can (10.5 ounces)	**cream of chicken soup,** condensed
I can (10.5 ounces)	**cream of mushroom soup,** condensed
I cup	**sour cream** or **plain yogurt**
I cup	**finely chopped green onion**
$^1/_2$ cup	**chopped green chiles**
3 cups	**grated cheddar cheese**
3 cups	**cooked cubed chicken**

Cut or tear tortillas into bite-size pieces. Combine soups, sour cream, onion, chiles, and half of cheese. Spread a little of soup mixture in bottom of a 9 x 13-inch pan. Layer with half of tortillas, chicken, and soup mixture. Repeat layer and top with remaining cheese. Bake 60 minutes at 325 degrees. Makes 6 servings.

MEXICAN CORN TORTILLA PIZZAS

I tablespoon	**vegetable** or **canola oil**
6	**corn tortillas**
I pound	**ground beef**
I	**small onion,** chopped
I envelope	**taco seasoning**
I can (16 ounces)	**refried beans,** heated
2 cups	**grated cheddar cheese**

Preheat oven to 350 degrees. In a large frying pan, heat vegetable oil. Place a tortilla in hot oil. Fry 20 seconds on each side. Remove tortilla from pan and blot with a paper towel to remove excess grease. Repeat for remaining tortillas. Arrange tortillas on 2 baking sheets.

Wipe excess grease from frying pan and brown beef and onion together until beef is done and onion is translucent. Drain, if necessary. Stir seasoning into meat. Spread a layer of refried beans over entire surface of each tortilla. Evenly divide meat mixture over tortillas. Sprinkle cheese over top. Bake 20 minutes. Garnish individual pizzas with diced tomatoes, green chiles, avocado, or sour cream. Makes 4–6 servings.

TORTILLA CHIP CASSEROLE

I pound	**ground beef,** browned and drained
I cup	**salsa**
$^1/_2$ cup	**sour cream**
2 teaspoons	**chili powder**
3 cups	**crushed tortilla chips**
2 cups	**grated cheddar cheese**
2 cups	**shredded lettuce**
I	**medium tomato,** chopped

Mix together ground beef, salsa, sour cream, and chili powder. Layer half of meat mixture, chips, and cheese. Repeat layers. Bake 20–30 minutes, or until bubbly, at 350 degrees. Serve topped with lettuce and tomato. Makes 6 servings.

CLASSIC BURRITOS

3 cups	**cooked and diced chicken** or **beef**
6	**large flour tortillas**
I can (30 ounces)	**refried beans**
3 cups	**grated cheddar cheese**
I cup	**salsa**
	guacamole
	sour cream
	salsa

Cook and season meat as desired. Place a tortilla in microwave 20–30 seconds, or until softened. Spread $^1/_2$ cup beans, $^1/_2$ cup cheese, $^1/_2$ cup meat, and a spoonful of salsa in a rectangle along one side of tortilla. Fold in sides and roll up burrito style. Garnish with guacamole, salsa, and sour cream. Makes 6 servings.

VARIATION: To make chimichangas, make burritos as directed above. Then heat some canola oil over medium heat in a frying pan. With tongs, place burrito seam-side down in oil and hold I minute. Release tongs and cook I–2 minutes, or until browned. Turn over and cook I–2 minutes more. Remove from oil and blot with paper towel.

CLASSIC ENCHILADAS

12 **corn tortillas**
$^1/_2$ cup **butter**
1 can (30 ounces) **enchilada sauce**
1 can (4 ounces) **tomato paste**
4 cups **grated cheddar cheese**

Preheat oven to 350 degrees. Cook 1 tortilla at a time in a small frying pan in about 1 teaspoon of butter until tortillas are soft and pliable. Mix enchilada sauce and tomato paste. Spread 1 cup of sauce mixture in bottom of a 9 x 13-inch pan. Roll $^1/_3$ cup cheese in each tortilla jelly roll style and place seam-side down in pan. Pour remaining sauce over top. Bake 30–40 minutes, or until bubbly. Makes 6 servings.

VARIATION: Use only half the cheese and add meat, such as chicken with green chiles, or shredded beef with jalapeños.

GREEN CHILE BURRITOS

2 pounds	**lean boneless pork roast,** cubed
2 tablespoons	**minced garlic**
I can (10 ounces)	**tomatoes and green chiles,** with liquid
I can (4 ounces)	**chopped green chiles**
	chili powder and salt, to taste
8	**medium flour tortillas**

Put pork and garlic in a lightly greased 4$\frac{1}{2}$- to 6-quart slow cooker. Cover and cook on low heat 8–10 hours, or on high heat 4–6 hours. Add tomatoes and green chiles and cook I hour more on high uncovered. Season with chili powder and salt. Place about $\frac{1}{2}$ cup mixture on each tortilla, roll up, and serve. Garnish with guacamole, sour cream, and/or salsa. Makes 6–8 servings.

TORTILLAS IN BLACK BEAN SAUCE

I can (15 ounces)	**black beans,** rinsed and drained
I can (19 ounces)	**enchilada sauce**
18	**corn tortillas**
1/2 cup	**butter**
I container or bag (12 ounces)	**queso fresco,** crumbled
I cup	**chopped cilantro**
2	**medium tomatoes,** chopped

Blend beans and enchilada sauce in blender until smooth. Saute each tortilla in a little butter until firm but not crisp. Spread tortillas, one at a time, with black bean sauce on one side. Fold in half and then in half again. Arrange 3 folded tortilla triangles on the center of each serving plate. Spread all 3 tortillas with more sauce. Microwave 1 1/2–3 minutes, or until heated through, and sprinkle with a little queso fresco, cilantro, and tomatoes. Makes 6 servings.

MOM'S WHITE ENCHILADAS

1/4 cup	**flour**
1/2 cup	**butter,** divided
3 cups	**chicken broth**
I can (12 ounces)	**diced green chiles**
I container (16 ounces)	**sour cream**
12	**corn tortillas**
	butter, for sauteing
I pound	**grated Monterey Jack cheese**
6 to 8	**green onions,** chopped

Preheat oven to 350 degrees. Cook flour in 1/4 cup butter in a large frying pan until golden brown; then add broth. Cook over medium heat until thickened, about 5 minutes. Remove from heat and stir in green chiles and sour cream. Spread I cup of sauce in bottom of a 9 x 13-inch pan and set the rest aside to cool.

Saute tortillas in remaining butter until firm but not crisp. Roll up 1/3 cup cheese and I tablespoon green onions in a tortilla jelly roll style. Repeat for remaining tortillas, placing each seam-side down in pan. Pour remaining sauce over top. Bake 40–50 minutes, or until bubbly. Makes 6 servings.

CLASSIC FAJITAS

$^1/_4$ cup	**lime juice**
I tablespoon	**soy sauce**
I tablespoon	**olive oil**
I tablespoon	**minced garlic**
I teaspoon	**white pepper**
I pound	**round steak,** sliced in $^1/_4$-inch strips
I	**yellow** or **purple onion**
I each	**red, green,** and **yellow peppers**
$^1/_2$ cup	**canola oil**
12	**medium flour tortillas**

Mix first five ingredients. Pour mixture over meat and marinate, covered, at least 4 hours or overnight. Cut onion and peppers into $^1/_4$-inch strips. Heat oil in large frying pan until very hot. Add meat and stir frequently. When meat loses its pink color, add onion and peppers. Saute until vegetables are cooked through but not limp. While sizzling, serve with flour tortillas to roll individually. Makes 6 servings.

VARIATIONS: Most meats and vegetables are excellent cooked in the same style as directed above. Possible combinations are shrimp or white fish fillets with mushrooms and onion, chicken strips with zucchini, or veggie fajitas with a variety of vegetables.

SPICY DOUBLE-DECKER TACOS

1 pound	**ground beef**
1 envelope	**taco seasoning**
1 can (10 ounces)	**diced tomatoes and green chilies,** with liquid
6 to 8	**taco shells**
6 to 8	**small flour tortillas**
1 1/4 cups	**grated cheddar cheese**
1 1/2 cups	**shredded lettuce**

In a frying pan, brown and drain ground beef. Stir in taco seasoning and tomatoes. Cover and cook over low heat 10 minutes. Place a flour tortilla inside each hard taco shell. Place a scoop of meat mixture into each flour tortilla. Sprinkle a small amount of cheese over meat, then put shredded lettuce over top. Garnish with salsa and sour cream. Makes 3–4 servings.

DESSERTS

CHERRY ENCHILADAS

I can (21 ounces)	**cherry pie filling**
6	**medium flour tortillas**
1/2 cup	**butter** or **margarine**
1/2 cup	**sugar**
1/2 cup	**brown sugar**
1/2 cup	**water**

Spread pie filling evenly down the centers of tortillas. Fold both ends over filling, then roll up jelly roll style to form enchiladas. Place seam-side down in a lightly greased 8 x 8-inch or 9 x 9-inch pan.

In a saucepan, melt butter. Add sugar, brown sugar, and water. Stirring constantly, bring mixture to a boil. Reduce to medium-low heat and simmer 2–3 minutes. Pour sauce over enchiladas.

Preheat oven to 350 degrees. Allow sauce time to return to room temperature before baking enchiladas. Bake 15–20 minutes, or until light golden brown. Serve warm with a scoop of vanilla ice cream. Makes 6 servings.

VARIATION: Any flavor pie filling may be substituted.

BANANA QUESADILLAS

1 package (8 ounces) **cream cheese,** softened
1/2 cup **sugar**
1 teaspoon **vanilla**
4 **bananas**
8 **medium flour tortillas**

Mix cream cheese, sugar, and vanilla. Mash 2 bananas and stir into cream cheese mixture. Spread 1/2 cup banana mixture on half of the tortilla. Place flour tortilla in a nonstick frying pan over medium low heat. Slice remaining bananas and add 5 to 6 slices over top of banana mixture. Fold plain half of tortilla over top, forming a half circle. Cook, turning about every 30 seconds until tortilla is light golden brown on both sides. Serve warm with cinnamon sugar, whipped topping, or caramel and chocolate sauce over top. Makes 6–8 servings.

CHOCOLATE RASPBERRY BURRITOS

2 cups	**semi-sweet chocolate chips**
2 cups	**fresh** or **frozen raspberries**
8	**medium flour tortillas**
4 tablespoons	**butter,** melted
4 tablespoons	**sugar**
2 teaspoons	**cinnamon**

Place $1/4$ cup chocolate chips and $1/4$ cup raspberries in the center of a tortilla. Fold edges in and roll up to form a burrito. Bake seam-side down on a baking sheet 20 minutes at 425 degrees, or until light golden brown. Remove from heat and brush with melted butter; then sprinkle with sugar and cinnamon. Makes 8 servings.

CINNAMON CRISPS

6	**small, medium,** or **large flour tortillas**
1/4 cup	**sugar**
1 teaspoon	**cinnamon**

Preheat oven to 400 degrees. Lightly sprinkle tortillas with water. Combine sugar and cinnamon, and sprinkle over tortillas. Cut each tortilla into 8 wedges. Place wedges in a single layer on lightly greased baking sheet. Bake 8–10 minutes, or until light golden brown and crisp. Serve with fruit salsa or your favorite fruit dip. Makes 3–4 servings.

TORTILLA CANNOLIS

canola oil, for deep frying
8 medium flour tortillas
1/3 cup sugar, mixed with
2 teaspoons cinnamon
1 cup ricotta cheese
1 cup sugar-free chunky fruit jam or
fresh pureed fruit
1 bag (16 ounces) chocolate chips, melted
whipped topping, for garnish

Heat oil in a deep fryer until very hot. Roll up a flour tortilla, leaving a
hollow center, and fasten with a toothpick. Deep fry until golden
brown. Remove from heat and, using tongs, roll immediately in sugar
mixture. Mix ricotta cheese and jam. Fill tortilla shell with cheese mixture.
Place on serving plate, drizzle with melted chocolate, and top with a
dollop of whipped topping. Makes 4–6 servings.

MEXICAN APPLE STRUDEL

6 cups **peeled and grated cooking apple**s
1 cup **raisins**
1 tablespoon **lemon juice**
1 cup **sugar**
1 tablespoon **cinnamon**
1 cup **chopped nuts**
8 **medium flour tortillas**
1/2 cup **butter,** melted

Mix apples, raisins, lemon juice, sugar, cinnamon, and nuts.
Microwave a tortilla 20 seconds to soften. Spread one cup apple
mixture on tortilla. Roll up jelly roll style. Wrap tightly with plastic
wrap and chill 1 hour. Remove plastic wrap and cut into 1 1/2-inch
slices. Place on baking sheet and secure with toothpicks. Brush
generously with butter. Bake 30 minutes at 350 degrees. Serve with
a dollop of whipped topping, if desired. Makes 6–8 servings.

DESSERT NACHOS
WITH FRUIT SALSA

Cinnamon Crisps (see page 113)
1 package (8 ounces) **cream cheese,** softened
$1/_4$ cup **orange juice**
4 cups **chopped fresh fruit,** such as strawberries, kiwi, peaches, mango

Arrange cinnamon crisps on a plate. Mix cream cheese and orange juice together. Drizzle cream cheese mixture over Cinnamon Crisps. Sprinkle fresh chopped fruit over top. Makes 4–6 servings.

SOUTHWEST BREAD PUDDING

3	**eggs**
3 cups	**milk**
$^1/_2$ cup	**sugar**
I teaspoon	**ground nutmeg**
I tablespoon	**ground cinnamon**
$^1/_4$ cup	**butter,** melted
I tablespoon	**vanilla**
$^1/_4$ cup	**raisins**
I cup	**chocolate chips**
8	**slices stale white bread,** torn into pieces (about 6 cups)
3	**medium flour tortillas,** torn into pieces (about 2 cups)

Mix eggs with a fork in a large mixing bowl. Add milk, sugar, spices, butter, and vanilla. Place remaining ingredients in a large mixing bowl and toss; then spread in a I $^1/_2$-quart baking dish. Pour egg mixture over top. Let stand 30–60 minutes. Bake 30 minutes at 350 degrees, or until golden brown on top. Remove from oven and sprinkle with additional sugar and cinnamon. Serve warm with a dollop of whipped topping or ice cream, if desired. Makes 8 servings.

LATTICE-TOP PEACH COBBLER

$^1/_4$ cup **butter**
$^1/_2$ cup **sugar**
2 tablespoons **flour**
1 tablespoon **cinnamon**
8 cups **sliced peaches***
4 **large flour tortillas**

Melt butter in a 2-quart casserole dish. Mix together sugar, flour, and cinnamon, and toss with peaches. Spread peaches on top of butter. Wet tortillas under running water. Place two tortillas together and cut into 1-inch strips. Weave over top of peaches, lattice-style. Repeat with remaining tortillas. Entire dish should be covered with tortilla strips. Bake 30–40 minutes at 350 degrees. Makes 6–8 servings.

*Drained canned peaches may be used in this recipe.

HOT FUDGE TOSTADA

4 **medium gordita-style flour tortillas**
cinnamon and **sugar**
6 cups **vanilla ice cream,** divided
1 jar **hot fudge ice cream topping**

Center tortilla in a microwave-safe cereal bowl. Press tortilla down to form the shape of the bowl. Microwave 30 seconds. Remove and press down air pockets that have formed. Microwave an additional 30 seconds. Remove tortilla and place on a tray where it can continue to dry out. Repeat process for remaining tortillas. Sprinkle cinnamon and sugar inside bottom of tortilla bowl. Place two or three scoops of ice cream in tortilla bowl. Heat hot fudge according to directions and drizzle over ice cream. Makes 4 servings.

STRAWBERRY MARGARITA SQUARES

Crust:

1 1/2 cups	**finely crushed tortilla chips**
1/4 cup	**melted butter**
1 tablespoon	**sugar**

Filling:

1 can (14 ounces)	**sweetened condensed milk**
2 cups	**pureed strawberries**
1/2 cup	**lime juice**
1 container (8 ounces)	**frozen whipped topping,** thawed

Mix crust ingredients together and press into a 9 x 13-inch pan. Mix first three filling ingredients together. Gently fold whipped topping into strawberry mixture and pour over top of crust. Freeze 4–6 hours. Let stand at room temperature 15 minutes before serving. Cut into squares and garnish with fresh sliced strawberries. Makes 10–12 servings.

STRAWBERRY SHORTILLA

1 1/2 cups **sugar,** divided
8 cups **sliced strawberries**
12 **medium flour tortillas**
1/4 cup **butter**
1/2 cup **sugar**
1 (8 ounces) container **whipped topping,** thawed

Add 1 cup sugar to sliced strawberries and let sit 20–30 minutes. Cut tortillas into 3- to 4-inch circles, using a small bowl as a guide. Saute each tortilla circle in 1 teaspoon butter until lightly crisp. Using tongs, remove from frying pan and sprinkle each side with 1 teaspoon sugar. Place one tortilla circle on a plate. Top with 1/2 cup strawberries. Place another tortilla circle on top and top with 1/2 cup more strawberries. Top with a large dollop of whipped topping. Makes 6 servings.

UPSIDE-DOWN APPLE PIE

$1/2$ cup	**butter**
$1/2$ cup	**brown sugar**
1 cup	**chopped pecans**
2	**large flour tortillas**
$1/2$ cup	**sugar**
$1/4$ cup	**flour**
1 teaspoon	**cinnamon**
6 cups	**tart apples,** peeled and sliced*

Preheat oven to 350 degrees. Spray an 8-inch pie pan with nonstick cooking spray. Line pie pan with wax paper. Mix $1/4$ cup butter, $1/4$ cup brown sugar, and pecans; spread over wax paper in bottom of pie pan. Place one tortilla over top. Combine rest of ingredients except remaining tortilla. Spread evenly in pie pan. Place tortilla over top. Press down to remove air pockets. Cut slits in tortilla. Bake 60–80 minutes, or until golden brown and heated through. Remove and cool 20–30 minutes. Invert onto a serving plate and remove wax paper. Serve immediately with ice cream, if desired. Makes 6–8 servings.

*Approximately 6 large apples.

S'MORES NACHOS

Cinnamon Crisps (see page 113)
1/2 cup **caramel sauce**
20 to 30 **mini marshmallows**
2 **chocolate candy bars,** broken into pieces
1 cup **graham cracker crumbs**

Spread Cinnamon Crisps on a 9 x 13-inch pan or oven-proof platter. Drizzle caramel sauce and sprinkle marshmallows and chocolate pieces over top. Place on center rack of oven and broil 3–5 minutes, or until light golden brown and bubbly. Remove from oven and sprinkle with graham cracker crumbs. Makes 4 servings.

NOTES

NOTES

NOTES

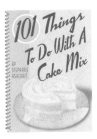

ABOUT THE AUTHORS

Stephanie Ashcraft was raised near Kirklin, Indiana. She received a bachelor's degree in family science and a teaching certificate from Brigham Young University. Stephanie loves teaching and spending time with friends and family. Since 1998, she has taught cooking classes and workshops. She and her husband, Ivan, reside in Rexburg, Idaho, with their children. Being a mom is her full-time job.

Donna Kelly was raised in Tucson, Arizona, and grew up on tortillas as a family staple. She is a southwest cooking fanatic, and especially enjoys the challenge of taking traditional recipes and giving them a southwest spin. Her other passion is fighting child abuse, and she currently works as a child abuse prosecutor. She and her very patient husband, James, live in Provo, Utah with their four delightful children: Kathleen, Amelia, Matthew and Jacob.